Pink T...

By Liza Charlesworth

ISBN: 978-1-339-02775-3

Art Director: Tannaz Fassihi; Designer: Tanya Chernyak
Photos © Getty Images and Shutterstock.com.
Copyright © Liza Charlesworth. All rights reserved. Published by Scholastic Inc.

1 2 3 4 5 6 7 8 9 10   68   32 31 30 29 28 27 26 25 24 23

Printed in Jiaxing, China. First printing, August 2023.

SCHOLASTIC

Do you think an animal
can be pink? It can!
A lot of things are pink.

This pig is pink.
It can run and jump.
It can sink in the mud.

This fish is pink.
It can swim in a tank.
Swish, dash, dunk!

This big bug is pink.
It can run and sit.
It can sing a song.

Can a moth be pink? Yes!
It has such soft wings.
It can drink from a plant.

This bird is pink.
It has long, thin legs!
It can grunt and honk.

Pigs and fish and big bugs!
Moths and birds with long legs!
Thanks so much for being pink.